Cruel and Tender

Martin Crimp was born in 1956. His plays include
Definitely the Bahamas (1987), *Dealing with Clair*
(1988), *Play with Repeats* (1989), *No One Sees the
Video* (1990), *Getting Attention* (1991), *The Treatment*
(winner of the 1993 John Whiting Award), *Attempts
on Her Life* (1997), *The Country* (2000) and *Face to the
Wall* (2002). A short fiction, *Stage Kiss*, was published in
1991 and *Four Imaginary Characters* appeared in 2000 as
a preface to *Plays One*. In 2004 the French and German
premieres of the short play *Fewer Emergencies* were
staged at the Théâtre National du Chaillot and the
Schaubühne in Berlin. He has also translated works by
Ionesco, Koltès, Genet, Marivaux and Moliére.

by the same author

MARTIN CRIMP PLAYS ONE
(*Dealing with Clair, Play with Repeats,
Getting Attention, The Treatment*)
THREE ATTEMPTED ACTS
(in *Best Radio Plays of 1985*)
NO ONE SEES THE VIDEO
ATTEMPTS ON HER LIFE
THE COUNTRY
FACE TO THE WALL *and* FEWER EMERGENCIES

translations

THE CHAIRS (Ionesco)
THE MISANTHROPE (Molière)
ROBERTO ZUCCO (Koltès)
THE MAIDS (Genet)
THE TRIUMPH OF LOVE (Marivaux)
THE FALSE SERVANT (Marivaux)

MARTIN CRIMP

Cruel and Tender

after
Sophocles' *Trachiniae*

ff

faber and faber

First published in 2004
by Faber and Faber Limited
3 Queen Square, London WC1N 3AU

Typeset by Country Setting, Kingsdown, Kent CT14 8ES
Printed in England by Mackays of Chatham plc, Chatham, Kent

A CIP record for this book
is available from the British Library

0-571-22495-4

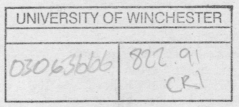
2 4 6 8 10 9 7 5 3 1

Cruel and Tender was commissioned by the Wiener Festwochen, the Chichester Festival Theatre and the Young Vic Theatre Company. It was first presented, in a co-production with the Théâtre des Bouffes du Nord and Ruhrfestspiele Recklinghausen, at the Young Vic, London, on 5 May 2004. The cast was as follows:

Laela Georgina Ackerman
Nicola Jessica Claire
The General Joe Dixon
Cathy Lourdes Faberes
James Toby Fisher
Amelia Kerry Fox
Jonathan Michael Gould
Iolaos Aleksandar Mikic
Rachel Nicola Redmond
Richard David Sibley
A Boy Stuart Brown/Mario Vieira

Direction Luc Bondy
Set Richard Peduzzi
Costumes Rudy Sabounghi
Lighting Dominique Bruguiere
Sound Paul Arditti
Wigs and make-up Cecile Kretschmar
Dramaturg Geoffrey Layton
Executive Producer Nicky Pallot
Casting Director Sam Jones
Assistant Director Lucy Jameson

Luc Bondy, fascinated by Sophocles' rarely performed
tragedy, encouraged Martin Crimp to produce a new
piece taking the original subject in a new direction
for his first English-language production.

Characters

Amelia, forties
The General, forties, her husband
James, late teens, their son
Richard, fifties, a journalist
Jonathan, thirties, a government minister

Amelia's three helpers
Housekeeper (Rachel)
Physiotherapist (Cathy)
Beautician (Nicola)

Two children from sub-Saharan Africa
Laela, eighteen
A Boy, about six

Iolaos, a friend of the General

Note on the Text

A slash like this / indicates the point of interruption
in overlapping dialogue.

The time is the present.
The place is the General and Amelia's
temporary home close to an international airport.

Part One

ONE

Amelia holds a white pillow. Her Housekeeper tidies the room.

Amelia
  There are women who believe
  all men are rapists.
  I don't believe that
  because if I did believe that
  how—as a woman—could I go on living
  with the label 'victim'?
  Because I am not a victim—oh no—
  that's not a part I'm willing to play—believe me.

She smiles.

  I was just fifteen
  living with my father
  living very very quietly with my father
  when the first man came to my father
  wanting me. He described to him
  the various ways he wanted me
  while I listened outside the door in the very short skirt
  and the very high-heeled agonising shoes
  I had begged and begged to be allowed to wear.
  I ran up to my room. Locked the door. Stopped eating.

She smiles.

  Three years later and I'm married—
  incredibly—to a soldier—
  to the only man
  who has ever remembered the colour of my eyes

after a single conversation under a tree.
I am eighteen years old and I have a house
a husband and a bed—
a bed with white pillows—
and a child.
I abandon my course at university
to become the mother of a child—
even if he—the father—
the soldier who is by now of course the great general—
only sees this child at distant intervals
like a farmer inspecting a crop
in a remote field.
Because my husband is sent out
on one operation after another
with the aim—the apparent aim—
of eradicating terror: not understanding
that the more he fights terror
the more he creates terror—
and even invites terror—who has no eyelids—
into his own bed.
And now those operations are over
instead of being respected for having risked his life
time and time and time again
he is accused of war crimes—murdering a civilian.
They say he dragged this boy off a bus
and cut his heart out in front of the crowd.
Which is why we were shipped out here
to the suburbs
close to the airport perimeter
and told 'Don't talk to the press' blah blah blah
while my husband vanishes—
is driven away in a black car
with black glass in the windows
and I'm told nothing—
nothing now for over a year.
Are you saying that's reasonable?

Housekeeper I'm not saying anything, Amelia: that's not my job. My job is to run the house—clean it—make sure the ironing's done and that the fridge gets regularly defrosted. Because I'm not here—I'm sorry, Amelia, but I'm not here to offer advice. Although if that *was* my job . . .

Amelia Oh?

Housekeeper Yes—if that *was* my job, I'd like to ask why you don't get that son of yours to do something— why can't James—why can't James find out where his father is?—he's old enough.

Amelia (*calls*) James.

Housekeeper Most boys his age are / working.

Amelia (*calls*) James. Come here.

Housekeeper Or studying. I mean what's wrong with him earning some / *money*?

Amelia (*calls*) James. I want you.

James appears, reluctantly. Pause.

James What is it, Mum? I'm busy.

Housekeeper Don't you dare talk to your mother / like that.

Amelia (*smiles*) Keep out of it, please. (*Slight pause.*) James?

James Yes?

Amelia Look at me when I talk to you. (*Slight pause.*) I SAID WILL YOU PLEASE LOOK AT ME.

He looks at her.

I want you to find out where your father is. (*Slight pause.*) I said: I want you to find out where your / father is.

James I know where my father is.

Amelia Oh? Where?

James (*imitating her*) 'Oh? Where?'

Housekeeper Don't talk to your / mother like that.

Amelia Keep out of it.

James He's in Gisenyi.

Amelia He's what?

James He's in a war-zone, Mum. He was supposed to be in Asia but they're saying he's now in Africa. They're saying he's been sent to Africa and is attacking or is about to attack the camp or the city or the whatever it's supposed to be of Gisenyi. (*Grins.*) Don't you read the papers? (*Pause.*) What's wrong?

Amelia See if it's true.

James What d'you mean, Mum, see if it's true?

Amelia Go there. See if it's true.

James Go there? It's a war-zone.

Housekeeper Do what you're told.

Amelia That's right—she's right—don't answer me back, James—just do what you're told.

   Slight pause.

James Mum?

Housekeeper I'll help him pack.

James Mum?

Amelia And he'll need a visa. What? What? Don't you love your father?

4

Housekeeper Don't you love your parents, James?

Amelia suddenly laughs and throws the pillow at James, who catches it.

James What's this for?

Amelia So you can sleep on the plane, sweetheart.

TWO

Amelia has cotton-wool between her toes. Her Beautician paints her toenails, while her Physiotherapist massages or manipulates her shoulders. Amelia is reading documents.

Physiotherapist How are you, Amelia? How're you feeling?

Beautician Says she's not sleeping.

Physiotherapist Oh? Not sleeping? Why's that?

Beautician Says she feels old.

Physiotherapist Well, she doesn't look old.

Beautician I keep telling her that.

Physiotherapist Tense though.

Beautician Mmm?

Physiotherapist Tense—very tense—very tense in the shoulders—very tense in the neck. Aren't you, Amelia.

Beautician She's not listening.

Physiotherapist She needs to relax more.

Pause.

What about exercise?

Beautician She doesn't go out.

Physiotherapist I meant the machine: aren't you using your machine?

Beautician She hates that machine.

Physiotherapist It's a good machine: it's one of the best there is. If you don't use your machine, Amelia, how d'you expect to sleep?

Beautician You mean she's not fit?

Physiotherapist I mean she's not tired: she's fit, but she's / not tired.

Beautician She's always tired: she never sleeps.

Physiotherapist Exactly my point.

Pause.

Well that's exactly the point I'm trying / to make.

Beautician She waits for the light.

Physiotherapist She ought to jog, she ought to be out there running, she ought to be taking more / exercise.

Beautician She waits for the light. She says she just lies there waiting for the light. She's depressed: she misses her / husband.

Physiotherapist Because I refuse to believe this is psychological.

Beautician Don't move, Amelia: it's still wet.

Pause. They move away and lower their voices.

Of course it's psychological: she's like a bird in a box— look at her.

Physiotherapist Like a what?

Beautician A bird—a bird in a box.

Physiotherapist You mean like a parrot?

Beautician I mean like a bird—like a wounded bird. Not like a parrot—like a bird / in a box.

Amelia
Please. Stop now. Don't try and sympathise.
You're not married
and you don't have children.
When you do have children
they'll break into your life
you'll see
like tiny tiny terrorists
who refuse to negotiate.
And when you have husbands
by which I mean men—
not these boys
not these boys who collect you on your nights off
and drive you in shirts ironed by their mothers
to the nearest multiplex
or back to their one-room flats that look out over
the lined-up trolleys in the supermarket car park
for the inept sex they've read about in magazines—
but men—hurt men—
men whose minds are blank
who fuck you the way they fuck the enemy—
I mean with the same tenderness—
when you understand that
then I will accept your sympathy.
(*Laughs.*) I'm sorry: I'm being cruel.
I'm very very pleased—yes—with my toenails:
   thank you
and if I've failed to use my exercise machine
'one of the best there is'—really?—
then I apologise.

Only these papers . . .
these papers are worrying me:
I found them in a drawer—
he's been—d'you see—look—last year—to a solicitor
and in case of his quote death
or mental incapacity unquote
gives power of attorney over his estate
'and over all things leased or assigned thereunto'
to James.
Which is odd not only because death
is not something he ever seriously considered
but also because—yes? what is it?

Housekeeper has appeared.

Housekeeper Someone to see you.

Amelia Well show them in. Because the fact is—
no—stop—wait—who?

Housekeeper A man with flowers.

Amelia
Flowers—good—show him in. But also odd because—
unless I'm not reading it properly—
and I obviously can't be reading it properly—
because the whole thing
this whole ridiculous document seems to be written
as if I no longer exist. (*Smiles.*)

Housekeeper has reappeared with Richard, a man in his fifties with a greying beard, holding a bouquet of flowers.

Richard Amelia?

Amelia Yes?

Richard Forgive me barging in like this but I have fantastic news. I was just at the press-conference and,

8

although details still have to be confirmed, what's clear is that the General has won some kind of decisive victory. (*Slight pause.*) They're saying it's a turning point.

Amelia I'm sorry? What 'press-conference'? What 'victory'? Who are you? Why did you let this man / into my house?

Richard I'm your friend, Amelia.

Amelia I don't have any friends with beards.

Richard My name is Richard. You once very kindly allowed me to interview you. We had lunch in a hotel.

Amelia Richard. Of course you are.

She smiles, kisses his cheek, takes the flowers.

What gorgeous flowers. (*to Housekeeper*) Put these in water / would you.

Richard The minister's still taking questions so I thought I'd get here first and bring you the good news. Any chance of a drink?

Amelia But why isn't he here?

Richard I've told you: he's taking questions. You know what journalists are like—probe probe probe—why do we always assume we're being / lied to?

Amelia My husband.

Richard I'm sorry?

Amelia Why isn't my *husband* here?

Richard Well he has to . . . secure the city, Amelia. There's very little—what's the word—infrastructure. (*Pause.*) Aren't you pleased?

Amelia Mmm?

Richard He's alive. Aren't you happy?

Amelia I'm very very happy. Thank you.

Richard Please don't cry. I wouldn't've come if I'd known this would / upset you.

Amelia I'm very very happy. And I'm very pleased you've come. Forgive me for crying.

She puts her arms round him and clings. He's embarrassed—doesn't know how to react.

Dance with me.

Richard I'm sorry?

Amelia Please. It's so long since I've danced.

Music: 1938 recording of Billie Holiday singing 'My Man'. They dance.

Voice of Billie Holiday
Sometimes I say
if I could just get away
with my man.
He goes straight
sure as fate
for it never is too late
for a man.

I just like to dream
of a cottage by a stream
with my man
where a few flowers grew
and perhaps a kid or two
like my man.

And then my eyes get wet I 'most forget
till he gets hot and tells me not to talk such rot.

Oh my man I love him so
he'll never know.
All my life is just despair
but I don't care.
When he takes me in his arms
the world is bright all right.

What's the difference if I say I'll go away
when I know I'll come back on my knees some day.

For whatever my man is
I'm his for ever more.

*As they continue to dance, the Housekeeper brings in
Jonathan—the minister—and with him two children
from sub-Saharan Africa: a girl of about eighteen and
a boy of about six.*

*Jonathan watches, then whispers to Housekeeper, who
turns off the music.*

Amelia Jonathan! How are you? How nice to *see* you!
(*Laughs.*) Who are these children?

Jonathan You seem very happy.

Amelia I *am* very happy—assuming it's true.

Jonathan Assuming what's true?

Amelia Well, the news of course. *Is* it true?

Jonathan Yes.

Amelia He's alive.

Jonathan Yes.

Amelia And unhurt?

Jonathan Yes.

Amelia I'm so relieved.

Jonathan Yes.

In the background Richard opens champagne and begins to fill glasses.

Well, yes, Amelia, I think we / *all* are.

Amelia (*laughs*) But who are these children? Are they *yours*?

Jonathan Do they look like my children?

Amelia Why did he bring his children? Have you been arguing with / your *wife*?

Jonathan These are not my children, Amelia. These are survivors.

Amelia Oh? (*Laughs.*) Survivors of what?

Richard (*raising glass*) Cheers.

Amelia Survivors of what?

Jonathan The only—in fact—apparently—survivors of your husband's assault. (*to Richard*) Cheers.

Amelia So why have you brought them to my house? I don't understand. Where is my husband? I want to see him.

Jonathan To see him? Well, listen, Amelia, it's a war—and—strictly off the record—while we are—and absolutely correctly are—claiming a military success—which—in military terms—don't misunderstand me—it most certainly is. Nevertheless the international community—as is its right—needs reassurance—it needs to be reassured that the General's actions were justified. And I'm happy to say that your husband—with the full backing I can assure you of this government—is putting up a robust and detailed defence.

The child-soldier thing has made our lives particularly difficult—since nobody likes killing children—whereas children themselves seem to find death and dismemberment one big joke. And of course the bus incident did your husband huge damage—although—in our opinion—the so-called child—terrorist, we would prefer to say—posed an immediate threat to our security to which the General responded in his own inimitable way.

Don't get me wrong, Amelia: we're thrilled—we're truly thrilled about what's happened. Because over the last year the General tracked that child back—he tracked that child back to the child's father. And what he discovered was that the father—a man called—yes?

Richard Seratawa.

Jonathan A man called—exactly—thank you—Seratawa—that Seratawa was using the camp—well not camp but city—was using the city of Gisenyi—is this right?— to recruit and to train terrorists—many of them, I'm sorry to say, children.

So what do you do? I'll tell you what you do, Amelia, you send in the General. You tell him to forget blue cards. You tell him to forget the conventional rules of engagement. Because if you want to root out terror—and I believe we all of us want to root out terror—there is only one rule: kill. We wanted that city pulverised—and I mean literally pulverised—the shops, the schools, the hospitals, the libraries, the bakeries, networks of fountains, avenues of trees, museums—we wanted that so-called city turned—as indeed it now has been—irreversibly to dust.

Now as for these children, the General found them in a drain, Amelia. And the General being what he is—what you and I both know him to be—I mean not just a soldier, but a man—and not just a man—a father—a husband. Being all those things, he has asked me—which is delicate, I realise—but asked me to bring these children who couldn't stand up for blood—who were slipping, Amelia, in that drain, barefoot on the blood, and on the pulverised bone of their brothers and sisters—has asked me to bring them to this house to remind us—to remind each one of us—of our common—I hope—humanity.

Pause.

Beautician They must be exhausted—look at them.

Housekeeper But where are they going to sleep? You can't just bring children into the house and expect / Amelia to—

Amelia Please. He's right. This is a very beautiful gesture on my husband's part, and I fully support it—is that understood? I want these children washed and given beds. I want them given thick sheets—cotton ones—white ones—and a light—they must have a light in the room— pink perhaps—and toys. Find them some of Jamie's old toys—but nothing frightening, please—no guns, no helicopters. And books. What kind of stories d'you like? (*Slight pause.*) I'm asking you a question, children. What kind of stories? (*Slight pause.*) Why won't they talk to me?

Jonathan You're distressed, Amelia. Why don't we deal with this / in the morning.

Amelia Distressed? I am not distressed, Jonathan, I am extremely happy. I simply want to know why they won't talk to me. I mean, the big one's obviously quite grown-up—aren't you—aren't you? What's your name? Why won't she talk to me?

Jonathan They don't read books.

Amelia Oh? Don't read books?

Jonathan No.

Amelia Then why did they have libraries?

Jonathan The libraries were used to conceal weapons.

Amelia You mean like the schools?—like / the fountains?

Jonathan Like the schools—yes. (*Slight pause.*) I am telling you the truth / Amelia.

Amelia Of course they read books—look at their eyes— they are intelligent. This one—this pretty one—look at her eyes. (*Slight pause.*) Or are you saying they don't speak English?

Jonathan They don't speak at all. They are unable to speak. They have been living in a drain, Amelia.

   Pause.

Amelia (*laughs*) Of course.

Jonathan Yes.

Amelia Forgive me.

Jonathan You are forgiven.

Amelia Please forgive me. So you don't think . . .

Jonathan Think what?

Amelia Nothing. (*to Girl*) Show me your tongue, sweetheart. Tongue. I want to see your tongue.

Jonathan Amelia?

   Amelia sticks her tongue right out over her lower lip and makes noises to encourage the Girl to show her tongue, if she has one. The Girl finally silently extends her tongue.

Amelia Thank god for that. (*Smiles.*) Well, thank god for that.

Everyone, except for the Girl, smiles. Amelia takes hold of her affectionately.

Listen: you are very welcome in this house. Whatever has happened to you, I want you to know that you are now safe, you are now loved. D'you understand me?

Amelia and the Girl stare at each other. The Boy suddenly breaks away and, before the Housekeeper can grab him, presses a button on the stereo. The Billie Holiday track plays from where it was interrupted to the end.

THREE

Night. Close, but not overwhelming, a plane passes on its way to the airport. Faint light reveals Richard sitting drinking. A beam of light enters the room and settles on Richard's face: it's the Housekeeper, with a powerful torch. Next to her is Amelia, carrying the Boy. On account of the child, they all speak softly.

Amelia Still here?

Richard Amelia? What're you doing?

Amelia He was having nightmares. We went outside to look at the stars, but there weren't any.

Richard Please. That hurts my eyes.

Amelia Switch it off.

Housekeeper Why haven't you gone home?

Amelia Switch it off. Take him, would you—he's getting heavy.

Housekeeper takes the child and gives Amelia the switched-off torch.

Richard I wanted to talk to you, actually.

Housekeeper makes to go.

Amelia No. Stay. Well here I am: talk to me.

Richard I thought you deserved to be told the truth.

Amelia Oh?

Richard Yes.

Amelia Deserved?

Richard Yes.

Amelia (*faint laugh*) What truth? What does a man like you know / about truth?

Richard He's lying.

Amelia Mmm?

Richard Jonathan—he's lying.

Amelia Of course he's lying—it's war—it's his job / to lie.

Richard He's lying about the children—not about the war—well, yes, of course about the war—but also about the children. Because these children are not what he said: 'victims'—'survivors'. They are the spoils, Amelia. (*Grins.*)

Amelia I don't understand.

Housekeeper He's drunk.

Amelia She's right—you're drunk—I want you / to leave.

Richard The oldest child—the girl—her name is Laela.

Amelia And?

Richard Give me the torch.

Amelia No.

Richard Give me the torch.

Amelia No.

A silent but intense struggle for the torch. Richard gets it, switches it on.

Richard Here come the helicopters. And here come the rockets out of the rocket-tubes. And here are the bottles of blood bursting in the hospital refrigerators. And oh—look—these are the patients blown off their beds onto the broken glass. And here are some heads on poles, Amelia . . .

Amelia Boring, boring—you think I don't / know all this?

Richard And here—oh look—what's this? What's this, Amelia? Who's this? Who's this girl? Her name is Laela. And he wants this girl so much—so much—he is so—what's the word?—inflamed—he is so—that's right—inflamed—that in order to take this girl from her father he is prepared to murder not just the father, but the inhabitants of an entire city . . .

Housekeeper Don't listen to him / Amelia.

Richard . . . of an entire city. Yes. Then ship the girl and what remains of her family . . . (*Shines beam at Amelia.*) . . . back to his own wife.

Pause. He snaps off the torch. The Boy whimpers.

Amelia What does he mean? What d'you mean? What're you trying to say to me?

Housekeeper (*to Boy*) Shh shh shh shh.

Richard (*grins*) Don't think telling you this gives me any pleasure.

Housekeeper (*to Boy*) Shh shh shh shh.

Amelia Get that child out, will you. Go on: *out*. Get it *out*.

The Housekeeper takes the Boy out.

Now. Explain.

Jonathan Explain what, Amelia?

Jonathan has appeared, mobile phone to his ear.

(*into phone*) Yup. Yup. I'm busy, sweetheart. Give me five more minutes, would you?

He ends the call but continues to scroll through messages without looking up.

Sorry—I'm needed elsewhere—explain what?

Amelia You're needed elsewhere.

Jonathan Yes—sorry—it's been one of / those nights.

Amelia I'm disappointed.

Jonathan Mmm?

Amelia I said: I'm disappointed—there were some questions I was hoping to ask.

Jonathan Questions—of course there are—why don't you call my office in / the morning?

Amelia Will you please look at me when I talk to you?

Jonathan Mmm?

He continues tapping at the phone, then looks up. He pockets the phone and smiles.

Amelia Who exactly are these children?

Jonathan Exactly? We're not in a position to say. They don't have papers.

Amelia But presumably they have names.

Jonathan Presumably their parents gave them names— I believe that is a universal habit. Why?

Amelia And who are their parents?

Jonathan I'm sorry?

Richard She's asking you who their / parents are.

Jonathan Their parents—I've explained this—are dead.

Richard Murdered.

Jonathan What?

Richard Their parents have been / murdered.

Jonathan Their parents have not been 'murdered', Richard—please grow up, please grow up—Seratawa was / a *terrorist*.

Richard So she's Seratawa's daughter.

Jonathan The children have no papers. Nothing at this stage can be confirmed. They were found—that's all—as I have already said—in a traumatised state—

Richard In a drain.

Jonathan Yes.

Richard Not in a palace, then.

Jonathan In a drain—in a palace—wherever they were found it was in a traumatised state, and I see no point in continuing / this conversation.

Richard Because I was told—oh, don't you? don't you?—because I was told they were found beneath a palace. I was told they were Seratawa's children.

Jonathan You were told.

Richard Yes, I was told by you. (*Slight pause.*) And I was also told—unless this was a smear—was this a deliberate smear?—because I was also told—as were others—that the General's objectives were not so much military, as sexual. That the assault—your word, not mine—was a sexual one.

Slight pause.

Jonathan You have a sick sick mind, my friend. Amelia, I think you've been distressed enough for one evening. I'll take / him home.

Amelia
  If you call me distressed
  Jonathan
  one more time
  or use my name
  Jonathan
  one more time tonight I won't scream
  no
  what I will in fact do
  is stuff your mouth with barbed wire.
  Because forgive me
  but I'm starting to find the way you speak
  an atrocity which makes cutting a man's heart out
  seem almost humane.
  If you have something to say
  about that child and my husband
  say it. But don't and I repeat
  don't think you can what?
  'spare my feelings?'

21

because I am not a child
and do not expect to be treated like a child
in my own house—is that clear?
You think it's a secret
that my husband has other women?
You think he doesn't tell me about them?
Oh yes—oh yes—he tells me about them—
their names
the colour of their hair—
because he knows I'd rather be told
even if being told is
and it is
I can promise you that it is
like having my face sprayed with acid.
When I slept with you
Jonathan
I told him the same evening
and after he'd punched his fist through the bathroom
    wall
he made me put on my red dress
and took me dancing.
Whereas—let me guess—you and
Kitty?—was that Kitty on the phone?—yes?—Kitty?—
Kitty and yourself—poor little Kitty
has never been told, has she,
even though her ignorance
is precisely what you despise about her—
am I right?

Slight pause.

You see
Jonathan
I happen to believe that love and truth
are the same thing.

Jonathan Your indiscretion appals me.

Amelia Oh, does it? I'm so sorry.

Jonathan All I am doing in a very very difficult situation here is trying to / protect you.

Amelia It's true, then.

Jonathan What?

Amelia What Richard says: what Richard / says is true.

Jonathan Nobody is trying to smear the General, no.

Amelia In other words it's true.

Jonathan (*to Richard*) You have no right to imply that.

Amelia Meaning it's true.

Jonathan Apparently.

Amelia I didn't hear you. What?

Jonathan I said apparently—yes—alright?—it's true.

Amelia bursts out laughing.

Amelia And you believe that?

Jonathan Yes.

Amelia That he would massacre a what?—an entire / *population*?—

Jonathan The evidence points that way.

Amelia 'The evidence points that way'—oh really?—does it?—for this *person*?—for this . . . *child*?

Richard Hardly a child, sweetheart.

Amelia stops laughing.

Jonathan Listen—

Amelia I don't believe it.

Jonathan Listen—

Amelia You're just trying to damage him—no.

Jonathan Amelia—

Amelia DON'T YOU DARE PUT YOUR HAND ON ME.

  Slight pause.

Jonathan (*calmly*) I have no wish to damage anyone—least of all yourself. I have to leave now. I suggest—and this is simply a suggestion—suggest that you go to bed—that you try to sleep—and that in the morning you call my office—excuse me.

  He turns away to answer his mobile.

Hello?
Where are you?
Uh-hu. Uh-hu. I see.
In the house.
I said in the house, I'm in the house.
(*meeting Amelia's eyes*) Asleep I think.
Uh-hu. Uh-hu. Okay. I'll try. One moment.

  He takes the phone from his ear.

It's the General.

Amelia (*overjoyed*) Well, give me the phone. Where is he? (*Slight pause.*) What's wrong with you? Give me the phone.

Jonathan He's on a plane. He's asking to speak to Laela.

Part Two

ONE

*Some days later, Laela, exactly like Amelia in the earlier
scene, is being given beauty treatment by the Beautician
and Physiotherapist. Following the words with her finger,
she reads aloud from a women's magazine.*

The Housekeeper plays quietly with the Boy.

Laela (*reads*) 'Tell him how you want to be touched. Tell
him what your . . .' (*Shows word.*)

Physiotherapist Fantasies.

Laela '. . . what your fantasies are. Don't feel . . .
ashamed. If your man doesn't touch you the way you
like, give your man a lesson. You may want to . . .'
(*Shows word.*)

Physiotherapist Masturbate.

Laela '. . . masturbate in front of each other. Many . . .'
(*Shows word.*) Couples?

Physiotherapist Very good.

Laela 'Many couples find this leads to better sex.
Remember there is no right or wrong. You are an . . .'
(*Shows word.*) . . . indian?

Physiotherapist Individual.

Laela '. . . an individual, and every . . . individual
expresses love in their own individual way.'

Beautician That's very good, Laela. Did you learn
English at school?

25

Laela Only boys go to school. I learn English at Tuseme club. (*Turns page.*) Oh, look at this dress! I want this dress!

Beautician What's Tuseme club?

Laela Tuseme club is HIV Aids learning club. You think he'll buy me this dress?

Physiotherapist Only if you're nice to him.

Laela Oh, I'm always nice to him.

The girls all laugh. Amelia appears. They go quiet.

Amelia What's that round your neck, Laela?

Physiotherapist You'd left it in the bathroom.

Amelia I've told you: she's not to take my things.

Housekeeper She doesn't mean any harm.

Amelia I'm sure. (*Smiles, holds out her hand.*) Laela?

After a pause, Laela unfastens the necklace she's wearing and gives it to Amelia. She continues to look at the magazine.

Don't you miss your family? (*Slight pause.*) I said: don't you miss / your family?

Laela My father was bad. He took the rice.

Amelia Oh?

Laela He took the rice out of people's mouths. And if he saw a man swallow the rice, he'd put his own hand into the man's body and pull the rice out again. (*Grins.*)

Amelia Your mother, then?

Laela I miss the General. When is he coming home? I want him to buy this dress.

Amelia The General is my husband, Laela. D'you understand what that means?

Laela One man can have many wives.

Amelia Of course, of course—but here—where you are now—when a man marries a woman, he stays with that woman.

Laela Just her?

Amelia That's what marriage is.

Laela (*laughs*) I don't believe you. That's what they tell girls at Tuseme club.

Amelia It's the truth.

Laela A man can have two wives under one blanket.

Amelia No. Not here. No.

Laela You mean he has to choose.

Amelia What I mean—Laela—is that the choice has already been made. I am his choice. I am the mother of his child. When he wakes up in the bed screaming, I am the person who switches on the light, and fetches the glass of water. (*Sees the Boy has a toy gun.*) What's this? I thought I said no guns. (*No one speaks.*) I said no guns.

Housekeeper It's only a toy, Amelia.

Amelia But I specifically / asked.

Laela (*soft*) Boys need to fight.

Amelia What did you say?

Laela (*with growing intensity*) Boys need to fight—they need to learn—they need to kill. Boys need to kill. Boys need to fight. Boys must fight. Boys must kill—must learn to kill. Boys need to fight—they need to learn—they need

27

to kill. Boys need to kill. Boys need to fight. Boys must fight. Boys must kill—must learn to kill. Boys need to—

Amelia hits Laela. Laela for a moment is stunned— then leaves the room. The Boy runs out after her.

Long pause. Housekeeper, Physiotherapist and Beautician watch Amelia, warily.

Suddenly Amelia points toy gun at Physiotherapist, who instinctively raises her arms. She smiles.

After we married—
did I ever tell you this?—
he was immediately sent away
into the desert
and I was bored.

She tosses gun into the toy-box.

I was so bored that I called
this boy I'd known at university
who'd spent his years at university
marching for peace
and when not marching for peace
shut in a lab. He was a chemist
and despised my husband.
Anyway I called him
and I said 'How are you?' he said
'I'm living in the country
come to the station and I'll collect you'
so I got the train
and he collected me from the country station
and without the beard
he was actually quite attractive.
I said 'This is a nice car, Robert' he said
'Yes, it comes with the job' I said
'What job?' he said 'I'll show you'.

She begins to unpick the stitches of a pillow.

So he drove me past these meadows
with rabbits and things—pheasants—
scuttling away to their holes
until we reached a beech-lined drive
which led to the facility
a kind of low concrete facility
a concrete and in fact windowless—yes—facility
where Robert
who'd spent his years at university
marching for peace
had been given a budget
staff and a number of caged dogs
and a number of caged primates
—macaques, were they?—
to develop weapons.

He showed me the park.
He knew the names of the wild flowers
flowers I hadn't even noticed
until he separated the grass where we were lying
and broke off the white stars.
I was so young! Next to the stream I did
of course I did the predictable things he wanted
except—because I was pregnant now—
let him touch me.

But the thing is
what I'm trying to say is
is on that day at the facility
he gave me this

She produces a glass tube the size of a pen-top.

which he said was his 'baby'.
He told me that this
whatever it is

chemical
that this chemical
his baby
took the will to fight out of a soldier
by making the soldier yearn for a safe place
making him feel the need of a safe place
an absolute need
for the love and the reassurance
of the person he was closest to.
Humane
was the word he used
to describe his baby.
I know it sounds mad
but I believed him
and two months later
he was found by that same stream
—how odd—
with his throat cut.

Slight pause.

(*Laughs.*) Don't look at me like that.

Housekeeper Like what, Amelia?

Amelia Like I'm out of / my mind.

Beautician It's probably just water. Show me.

Physiotherapist Does it smell?

Beautician It smells of scent.

Amelia That's from the drawer. I keep it in my perfume drawer.

Beautician How does it open?

Amelia It doesn't: you have to break the glass.

Housekeeper And he called it humane.

Amelia Yes. Why not?

Physiotherapist Weird.

Slight pause.

Beautician Amelia. Catch.

Beautician tosses the tube to Amelia who—terrified—catches it.

Amelia Idiot.

Housekeeper, Physiotherapist and Beautician laugh. Ignoring them, Amelia carefully inserts the tube inside the pillow.

Jonathan appears.

Jonathan What's the joke, ladies?

Amelia Come here.

Jonathan Oh?

Amelia Come here. Come on. Closer. Closer.

She kisses him at length. As she does so, Laela appears, holding a wet flannel to her face, and watches like the others.

Jonathan And what have I done to deserve that?

Amelia You're going to be my messenger.

Jonathan Oh? What's the message?

Amelia You're going to explain how nice I've been to the children—particularly to Laela.

Jonathan Uh-hu.

Amelia Because you've seen—you've all seen—yes?—how generously I've accepted the situation.

Jonathan Uh-hu. And?

Amelia And nothing.

He tries to move away. She stops him.

Oh yes: one other thing.
You're flying out to the camp
to pin medals on the boys
and to support my husband—yes?
Well listen
to remind him of home
to help him sleep before he finally comes home
I have a white pillow
I want you to take out to him.
Tell him to think of me.
Tell him to push his face
into the soft part of the white pillow
and his mouth
and his tongue
tell him to push his whole face into the white pillow
    until
he feels something smooth and hard inside the white
    pillow
snap.

Slight pause.

Will you do that, Jonathan?

Jonathan It will take up space.

Amelia His tongue?

Jonathan The pillow, Amelia.

Amelia You have power. *Make* space.

*During the preceding speech she has allowed Jonathan
to touch her. Now she gently removes his hand.*

Music: 1936 recording of Billie Holiday singing
'I Can't Give You Anything But Love'.

The messenger
Jonathan
must not be distracted from the message.

TWO

Evening. Music from previous scene continues uninter-
rupted as Housekeeper, Physiotherapist and Beautician
prepare the room for the General's return. They fill the
room with flowers, maybe put up a banner reading
'WELCOME HOME OUR HERO', and prepare a table for
Amelia and the General to eat together.

Voice of Billie Holiday
  I can't give you anything but love
  baby.
  That's the only thing I've plenty of
  baby.
  Scheme a while
  dream a while
  you're sure to find
  happiness
  and I guess
  all those things you've always pined for.

  Gee I'd like to see you looking swell
  baby.
  Diamond bracelets Woolworth's doesn't sell
  baby.

  Until that lucky day
  you know darn well
  baby
  I can't give you anything but love.

Amelia enters in the red dress she mentioned earlier. Her hair is elegant. She inspects the room. She turns off the music.

Amelia Zip me up will you.

Beautician attempts to zip up the dress.

Oh by the way
I think something's happened to one of the children.
Yes I think
well no not think I know
that something's happened to one of those children.
I told them not to touch my things.
You heard me—didn't you—say that
say 'don't touch my things'.
But one of them's been in my drawer
been poking their fingers into my perfume drawer
had all my perfume out
had the whole drawer out and / broken it.

Housekeeper Wrong with them?

Amelia What?

Housekeeper You said something happened?

Amelia Hurry up with this zip can't you?

Beautician It's tight.

Amelia It's meant to be tight—it's a / tight dress.

Housekeeper Happened to who? Laela?

Amelia What? No. The little one. It got something on its fingers and stopped breathing—you're hurting me.

Beautician Sorry.

Physiotherapist Stopped breathing?

Amelia You're hurting me—be careful.

34

Physiotherapist What d'you mean it / stopped breathing?

Amelia Oh nothing, nothing—leave me alone!

The zip is finally done up. Amelia smoothes the dress over her hips.

I told you:
one moment it was poking around in the drawer
and the next it momentarily
just momentarily stopped breathing.
It's fine—it's had a strawberry yoghurt—
it's watching TV—it's fine—
Laela washed its hands
and put it in front of the TV
with a packet of crisps and a yoghurt
and it's absolutely fine—I swear to you.
And of course we've looked in the drawer:
Laela's looked—I've looked—we've both—
well of course we've both of us
had that drawer completely to pieces
and looked and looked
but apart from the splinters of wood
there's nothing—Laela agrees—
she agrees with me
there's nothing in the drawer that could've made this
   happen.
So why should I feel afraid?
Mmm?
I have to ask myself—you see—
exactly why this thing this
whatever it is this
coincidence—yes—obviously—but why this
coincidence is frightening me.
And of course once I start asking myself that question
I start thinking about Robert and Robert's friends:
all Robert's friends at university

with their tobacco tins.
I keep seeing the little shreds
of dry tobacco in their tobacco tins
and the grey light in the stairwells
of their squatted apartments where they planned
—what?—to 'overthrow the state'
'kill the pigs' blah blah blah
'liberate'—by which they meant fuck—
women—all that shit—all that liberate
liberate and overthrow the state shit
so that when a banker got shot say
taking his kids to school
or if an army officer
burned alive in a nightclub explosion
or if some boy
some soldier even younger than they were
who had been defending their right
to despise their expensive education
came home on TV in a body-bag
that didn't even contain his whole body
they'd find that oh yes they'd find that not just
acceptable
but exhilarating.
So what if Robert never grew up?
What if he'd cut his hair and taken that job
out of perversity?
What if for him this word 'humane'
was a sick joke?
(*Smiles.*) Tell me I'm wrong.
Tell me he didn't calculate that one day
he would make me responsible for treating my
    husband
like a monkey in an experiment.

Housekeeper Well of course you're wrong.

Amelia What time is it?

Physiotherapist Nine.

Amelia Who's called? Has anyone called?

Housekeeper You're tired. You're imagining things.

Amelia Oh am I?

Housekeeper Of course you are.

Amelia You see that is exactly what I would *expect* to be told by a person with no imagination.

James Nice dress, Mum.

Amelia Jamie?

James has appeared, holding the pillow he took when he left: now dirty and torn. Amelia puts her arms round him. James does not respond.

(*Smiles.*) Look at you. I thought you were your father.

James No Mum, I'm not my father.

Amelia Don't you think? Doesn't he look exactly like / his father?

Housekeeper Where is your father, Jamie?

James Delayed. (*Grins.*)

Slight pause.

Shall we eat something?

Amelia I'm sorry?

James I said shall we eat something, Mum—I'm / hungry.

Amelia What's wrong with you? What's wrong with your eyes?

James I'm hungry. I've been travelling. I'd like to eat. Nothing's wrong with my eyes—I'm just tired and hungry. (*Grins.*) Nice dress.

37

Slight pause.

Amelia You just / said that.

James Maybe a bit tight.

Amelia What?

James Tight. Maybe a / bit tight.

Amelia That's the style. It's a tight style.

James It's a tight style.

Amelia Yes.

James Wine?

Amelia What?

James Wine?

Amelia Yes please.

They have sat at the table, James taking the place intended for his father. He pours Amelia a glass of wine.

James Well, come on, Mum—drink it.

Amelia Aren't you having any?

James Come on.

Housekeeper Ignore him, Amelia.

James I beg your pardon?

Beautician Leave your mum alone, James.

James Fuck off, bitch.

Amelia Jamie?

James Don't you tell me what to do in my own house.
I want all three of you out of this room now and I want

you to take that pillow and I want you to fucking clean it.
Go on—out. Drink the wine, Mum. (*She begins to drink.*)
All of it.

*As Housekeeper, Physiotherapist and Beautician leave
the room, Amelia drinks the glass of wine. James
immediately refills it.*

Well don't you want to hear about Africa?

Amelia Of course I do—how was / Africa?

James Africa? Africa was great, Mum. On Sunday
mornings the church bells ring and all the Africans get
into their African jeeps and drive to church under the
autumn leaves.

Amelia Oh?

James And in the afternoons—what?—does that surprise
you?—because in the afternoons, while their parents are
assembling flat-pack African furniture with hexagonal
keys, the kids hang out in the Mexican restaurants or
experiment with sex or with rocket-propelled grenades—
more wine, Mum?

Slight pause.

Amelia I didn't realise that they—

James That they what, Mum? Had Mexican food?

Amelia Had autumn—had autumn leaves.

James You see, at first I blamed the Mexican cuisine.
Because I wake up and I can hear Dad vomiting in the
bathroom and naturally I think it's the Mexican cuisine,
Mum—that Tex-Mex African pizza—that snake-meat
enchilada dished up at the victory celebration in the
officers' canteen—but no. No, Mum—it's not the food—
that's not why my father—who can walk into fire,

remember—walk into fire to drag out a wounded soldier and walk with that wounded soldier on his back for ten hours across sand—that's not why my father is in that bathroom gripping both sides of the sink the way an old man trying to get to the post office holds on to his walking-frame. That's not why he's sucking in air—sucking and sucking in the air, Mum, like he's drowning in his own spit.

And there's this thing on his back, Mum—no—not on his back but under it—this thing under his skin—like an animal under his skin—it's crawling—it's crawling under his skin—like an animal, Mum, trying to slide out from underneath—which is the chemical—the animal under the skin—the pain—the chemical—the thing your friend brought—the gift—the gift / your friend brought—

Amelia He's not my friend. / Stop this.

James —the gift of pain—the chemical—your chemical under the skin. (*Slight pause.*) And when he turns round it's his eyes—it's worked its way up his spine and into his eyes—he's got these eyes like a cat in the sun—pin-point eyes—he isn't human, Mum—that's what you and your friend have done to him—

Amelia Stop it.

James —not even human. Which is why when he talks to me—when he says 'It's going dark: give me your hand'—when he says 'Help me, help me, give me your fucking hand' there is no way I am going to let this person—no—sorry—thing—no way I am going to let this thing with the pin-point fucking eyes that used to be my dad even *touch* me.

Then it's TV drama, Mum. It's straight-to-video medical-emergency bullshit:
   'Chemical attack' blah blah blah.

'Atropine ten milligrams.'
'Oxygen.'
'Ventilate.' (*He grins.*)

So perhaps you would like to finish this glass of wine and explain to me why you have killed my father.

He pours wine into the glass, making it overflow. Amelia tries to stop him. The bottle falls onto the table.

Laughter: Housekeeper, Physiotherapist and Beautician, dressed up for an evening out, can be seen leaving the house.

Beautician (*calls*) 'Night, Amelia! 'Night, Jamie!

Housekeeper (*calls*) Back door's locked. Remember those children are still watching TV. Amelia?

Beautician Don't bother—she's not listening.

Physiotherapist Love those shoes.

Beautician Found them in her wardrobe—don't / tell anyone.

Housekeeper (*calls*) Make sure those children / get to bed.

Physiotherapist Let's just get out of here. Come on. Sweet dreams, Jamie.

Beautician Shh. Stop it.

Laughing and joking, the three women leave. Pause. James continues to stare at Amelia.

Amelia (*softly*) Nicola? Rachel? (*louder*) Rachel? I want you.

James They've gone, Mum.

Amelia (*calls out*) I want this mess cleared up. I want these things put away immediately. Rachel! Cathy!

James There's nobody here—they all / went out.

Amelia (*calls out*) Nicola! Rachel! Clear up this mess!

James They've left, Mum. There's nobody here. I am waiting for your / explanation.

Amelia Africa sounds lovely. I hope you took photographs. I'd love to see those leaves—and all the restaurants—I'd no idea—I thought it was all idleness and destruction—(*Calls.*) Laela?

James You know nothing, Mum: and that is because your life is entirely devoid of content. You don't even leave / the *house*.

Amelia (*calls*) Laela!

James It's like you live in a / *bunker*.

Amelia Laela! Turn off that / television and come in here!

James Africa? It's not Africa that's idle and destructive, Mum, it's you. Don't you understand / what you've done?

Amelia (*smiles*) Sweetheart. There you are. I'd like you to meet my son.

Laela has appeared. Slight pause.

Well, come on. Come on, Laela: meet my son.

She grips Laela's hand and pulls her into the room.

Laela, this is James. Jamie, this is Laela. What d'you think, James? As a man. Is she worth it? You don't need to look so blank—I'm asking you if she's worth it—well?

James You're hurting her.

Amelia Is that right? Am I hurting you, sweetheart?

Laela No.

Amelia You see: Laela says no. Laela's used to pain. She's used to dismemberment and death. Laela doesn't need you to explain to me how Laela feels. Do you, Laela?

Laela No.

Amelia How d'you feel, Laela?

Slight pause.

Laela I feel good.

Amelia You see: Laela feels good. So what d'you say, Jamie? Worth it? Come on. You're a man. You can judge. How many people would *you* kill?

James I don't understand. Who are you? What's she doing / in the house?

Amelia Don't you? Don't you? Well maybe you're not a man at all then. What do *you* say, Laela? Is this a man? Is it? A person who thinks it's—what?—brave is it, to come here and terrorise his mother? A person who is too frightened—by his own admission—Laela—is too frightened to take his *own dying father's hand*?

James backs away.

No—Jamie—I'm sorry—I'm very very sorry—please— please—that was wrong of me—please.

James goes out. In the silence, a plane passes. Then:

Laela I turned off the TV.

Amelia Mmm?

Laela I turned off / the TV.

43

Amelia Thank you, Laela.

Laela I'm sorry about the drawer.

Amelia The drawer doesn't matter.

Laela I will punish the boy.

Amelia Did he eat his yoghurt?

Laela Yes, but he spit out the fruit.

Amelia Spat, Laela—spat out the fruit.

Pause.

Can you drive a car?

Laela Can I . . .?

Amelia Drive. Can you drive a car?

Laela No.

Amelia Neither can I. If we could drive a car, we could drive to the airport. We could go shopping at the airport. What d'you think?

Laela Buy shoes.

Amelia We could buy shoes. We could buy luggage on wheels.

Pause.

What have I done, Laela?

Laela What have you . . .?

Amelia DONE. WHAT HAVE I DONE?

Pause.

Laela Can we really go to the airport?

Amelia Of course we can, sweetheart. But first you're going to pour me a glass of wine. Let's have a glass of wine together, shall we? Then what we'll do is we'll take the General's car and we'll drive to the airport and meet the General—yes? The two wives will drive to the airport in their husband's car to collect their husband from the airport—what d'you think? Good idea? Everybody drives—it can't be / difficult.

Laela It's broken.

Amelia Even really stupid stupid people drive a car— what?

Laela These glasses / are broken.

Amelia Then fetch some more.

Laela goes out.

I know what we can do, Laela:
how about we put ourselves—mmm?—
through the machines—
what d'you say?
How about we lie down on the rubber track
and ask to be X-rayed
because obviously
there's obviously something inside of us
Laela
some sharp object
some spike
something inside of us
a prohibited object we didn't know about
but that will show up on the screen close
because I think it must be very close to our hearts
—don't you think?—that spike?
So they'll ask us to strip.
And when we've stripped
(which I hope we will do like grown-ups without
    complaining)
one of those women with a rubber-glove

45

will push her hand
like a midwife Laela
will push her hand deeper and deeper into us
until the tip of her finger rests
just so
on the spike.

Laela reappears, holding glasses.

And she'll say
'I suspect you of terror.
You have a concealed weapon.
I can feel it next to your heart.'
'Oh really?' I'll say 'D'you mean love?'
And she'll say 'Not love
no
I'm talking about this spike.
Have you concealed this spike deliberately?
Or could it have been placed there
without your knowledge?'
And I'll lie to her
I'll say 'Deliberately of course.'
Because otherwise
I could be mistaken for a victim
and that's not a part
Laela
that I'm prepared to play.

*Amelia clenches her fist around one of the shattered
wine-glasses on the table and squeezes as hard as she
can. When she finally opens it, some of the glass drops
out, some remains sticking to her hand.*

(*Smiles.*) Let's look for the car keys. We're driving to the
airport.

Part Three

ONE

A month later. Saturday morning.

Beauty treatment: the Housekeeper is having the finger-nails of her right hand painted by the Beautician, while the Physiotherapist sits apart, leafing through a women's magazine.

There's a new object in the room: a small stainless-steel trolley containing items (cotton-wool pads, bottle of alcohol, medication, towels, thermometer, plastic gloves etc.) to care for an invalid. Perhaps also a bowl of fruit.

Housekeeper
Hairbrush.
Lamp.
Light-switch.
Doors—naturally.
The bed.
Bathroom mirror.
Bathroom sink.
Bathroom towels.
Telephone.
Medicine cabinet and all inside the medicine cabinet—
naturally.

Beautician (*faint laugh*) That's revolting.

Housekeeper
Well, you asked.
Jewellery box.

Beautician Don't.

Housekeeper
Jewellery box.
Toothbrush.

Physiotherapist Toothbrush?

Housekeeper
Toothbrush: that's what I said.
Toothbrush.
Hairbrush.
The bed.
The pillow.
Nightdress under the pillow—pure silk—ruined.
Oh, and underwear.
The underwear drawer.
Edge of the kitchen table.
Wall of the passageway.
Door—naturally—door to the garage.
Garage light-switch.
Wall around the light-switch.
Car windscreen.
The inside as well as the outside of the glass.
Car keys.
Mirror.

Pause. She examines her free hand.

What are these ridges in my fingernails?

Beautician Stress does that. They grow out.

Housekeeper I hope so.

Physiotherapist So you had to clear it all up?

Housekeeper What? The blood? No. That's what I'm saying. They told me to leave it. 'Don't touch anything. This is a crime scene.'

Physiotherapist Even the toothbrush?

Housekeeper Well exactly—it's not a crime to brush your teeth—it's not a crime to be broken-hearted. Is it?

Beautician Keep your hand still.

Housekeeper Well, is it? And they're asking me where I've been—why wasn't I in the house? And I say, 'Well it's my night off.' And they go, 'Just tell us where you've been.' So I tell them where I've been: I've been to the Star of Izmir. 'What's that?' So I explain it's an all-night Turkish restaurant close to the North Terminal, hotbed of international terrorism.

Physiotherapist (*laughs*) You didn't.

Housekeeper I most certainly did, Cathy—because these people are starting to make me very angry. They're all over the house like flies on a plate of ham, and of course I've got Jamie acting more like a six-year-old than an adult, blaming himself as if that that was any use because they'd had some kind of argument about the thing that happened to his father and he'd stormed out apparently and left her. Is this finished? (*i.e. nails*)

Beautician Uh-hu.

Housekeeper (*getting up and admiring her fingernails*) Because he's the one you see who saw the light on in the garage windows—I really like this colour: thank you—he saw the light on but it wasn't until he realised she was running the engine that it dawned on him what might be happening.

Slight pause.

What is this colour called?

Beautician 'Spangled Night.'

Housekeeper It's lovely.

Physiotherapist He looks nice in a suit, though.

Housekeeper I'm sorry?

Physiotherapist Jamie—looks really nice in / a suit.

Housekeeper He's certainly had some growing up to do, if that's what you mean.

   Pause.

Beautician So what is it they're talking about in there?

Housekeeper (*lowers voice*) What they're talking about is responsibility. Not about suits, Cathy, but about assuming responsibility. (*softer and softer*) And I would ask both you girls to remember that as far as we are concerned . . . this is a *perfectly normal day*. Understood?

   Offstage the General can be heard approaching, half speaking, half singing.

I am asking you if that is understood.

Beautician Normal day. Fine.

Housekeeper Cathy? (*Slight pause.*) Cathy?

Physiotherapist Yes alright, it's a normal day.

General (*off, sings/speaks without expression*) 'I can't give you anything but love—baby. That's the only thing I've plenty of—baby. Scheme a while. Dream a while. You're sure to find—happiness—and I guess—'

   The General appears, dressed in a tracksuit, and halts mid-phrase. The women look at him warily. He surveys the room. He smiles.

Ladies. Good morning.

Housekeeper *and* **Beautician** Good morning, General.

Physiotherapist How are you today?

General I feel good.

Pause. Without moving, he continues to survey the room.

Housekeeper D'you need emptying, General?

General Do I need what?

Housekeeper (*softly*) Empty his bag, Nicola.

General (*to Housekeeper*)
Now listen:
tell Amelia we're having lunch at the Chinese Embassy
then at three o'clock
put this in the diary
because at three o'clock
I'm talking to the minister about helicopters
because there are not enough helicopters
and I have men dying because of it and then at half
   past four
this should be in the diary
at half past four I am appearing on television
until half past five when a car is taking Amelia and
   myself
and make sure this car is booked
because we need to go directly to the airport
for a meeting at the United Nations in New York.
So you will kindly tell Amelia
that after lunch at the Chinese Embassy
she must come home and pack
and I will need the adaptor for my razor
because the voltage in New York is not the same is it?

Slight pause.

I am asking you a question.

During the preceding speech Beautician has wheeled the trolley over to the General, knelt to pull down his jogging-pants, revealing a urine-bag strapped to his leg, drained the bag into a jug and pulled the pants back up again. On his last line he grips her by the hair.

Beautician What question, General?

General What is the voltage in New York?

Beautician You're hurting me.

General I'm doing what?

Housekeeper (*calmly*) Let go of her hair. Please. She doesn't know the answer.

General (*releasing her*) Doesn't know the answer.

Beautician No—sorry.

General I've hurt you.

Beautician I'm used to it.

General Pain?

Beautician Yes.

General (*smiles*) Used to pain? Oh really?

Slight pause.

And you are . . .?

Beautician You know who I am. I'm Nicola.

General You're fucking my son.

Beautician No.

General You're the one fucking my son.

Beautician No.

General Which one of you is fucking my son, then?

Slight pause. He looks at them. Points at Physiotherapist.

This one.

Housekeeper (*to distract him*) Three o'clock, General?

General This is the one: look at her.

Housekeeper Three o'clock? Yes?

General This is the one. This is the one who shrieks in the night—like a fox—shrieks like / a fox.

Housekeeper Three o'clock?

General What?

Housekeeper At three o'clock you're talking to the minister—remember—about / helicopters.

General
At three o'clock I'm talking to the minister
that's right
about helicopters because there are not enough
helicopters and at half past four
put this in the diary
I am appearing on television until—

The General experiences an intense pain which momentarily stops him speaking. To master the pain he counts back in sevens:

One hundred and three . . . ninety-six . . . eighty-nine . . . eighty-two . . .

Physiotherapist General?

Beautician Keep back—don't touch him.

General . . . seventy-five . . . sixty-eight . . . (*Pain eases.*) sixty-one . . . and so on . . . (*Smiles.*) to infinity.

Slight pause.

Get me my son. I want to see my son—where is he?

Housekeeper James can't come. He's busy.

General I want to talk to him.

Beautician He's in a meeting.

General (*amused*) My son is in a meeting? What meeting?

Housekeeper Nicola just means there are people he has to / talk to.

General GET ME MY SON.

> *Housekeeper gestures to Physiotherapist, who leaves the room.*

(*paranoid*) Where's she going?

Housekeeper She's gone to get James.

General She's going to talk to the government.

Housekeeper She's gone to find James, that's all.

General Don't let her talk to / the government.

Beautician (*to distract him*) Shall we tidy you up, General? Mmm? Shall we make you look nice?—for the television?

General (*stares at her*)
D'you think I'm a child, Nicola?
Or maybe you think
is this what you think?
that I'm losing my mind?
that a chemical has made me lose my mind?
that because of that bitch
I felt the glass crack in the white pillow

54

is this what you think?
that the glass cracked in the white pillow and I lost
my mind? Because I wake up on a Saturday morning
smelling of my own shit
that makes me an imbecile?

James appears in suit, unseen by the General.

Well, does it? (*Smiles.*) Maybe you'd like me to call for
fire, Nicola.

Beautician Don't know what you mean.

General
  Call for fire
  give your co-ordinates and call for fire.
  Then you won't doubt the accuracy of my mind.
  Because my mind is accurate to one square metre
    anywhere
  on the surface of this earth.
  And if I call for fire
  Nicola
  you will quite simply turn into a stick of flame.

*Attack of pain. General counts as before. James
indicates to Housekeeper and Beautician to leave.
They go out.*

One hundred and five . . . ninety-eight . . . ninety-one . . .
eighty-four . . . seventy-seven . . . (*Pain eases.*) seventy-
seven . . . seventy . . . sixty-three—

James (*cold*) What d'you want, Dad?

General Mmm?

James What is it you want?

General (*simply*) I want you to find me the bitch.

James What bitch, Dad?

55

General The bitch that did this to me—the bitch that poisoned me—bring the bitch here.

James I'm not listening, Dad.

General Bring the bitch here. I want to break her legs.

James Don't use that word about my mother.

General Break her legs for me. I want to see her dance.

James I've told you: she's dead.

General Poison her the way she poisoned me.

James I've told you: she's dead.

General *Then* watch her dance—let's see her try and dance.

James You have seen her buried: you stood next to me.

  Pause.

General Died how?

James I've told you this.

General Killed.

James Yes.

General (*paranoid*) Killed by the government—murdered by the government.

James No, Dad—killed herself.

General Murdered by the government.

James Will you please listen to me: Amelia is dead. She killed herself. She killed herself because of you.

General (*smiles, flattered*) Me? Oh? Because of me?

James You have known this for a month now.

Pause. James makes to leave.

I'm sorry, Dad, but I have to go.

General Back to your meeting.

James What?

General You have to go back to your / meeting.

James Who told you that?

General Who are you talking to?

James I'm not talking to anyone.

General You're talking to the government.

James I talk to who I like, Dad. I live in this house and I talk to who I like and there is something you need to understand: you are a criminal. You are accused of crimes. You have wiped people off this earth like a teacher rubbing out equations. You've stacked up bodies like bags of cement.

General (*smiles*) Is this what you learn at the university?

James I'm not listening, Dad.

General To hate your father—to spit in your own / father's face.

James I said I'm not / listening.

General
　Because I have purified the world for you.
　I have burnt terror out of the world for people like you.
　I have followed it through the shopping malls
　and the school playgrounds
　tracked it by starlight across the desert
　smashed down the door of its luxury apartment
　learned its language
　intercepted its phone calls

smoked it out of its cave
thrown acid into its eyes and burned it to carbon.
While you've been logged on to internet chat-rooms
I've seen my friends burst open like fruit.
While you were hiding your face in that girl's hair—
yes?—yes?—
I have been breathing in uranium.
Every streak of vapour in a cold sky
is a threat
every child with no shoes
wandering up to a checkpoint
every green tree-line
every quiet evening spent reading
is a threat
and even the lamp on the bedside table
even the coiled filament inside the lamp
is a threat.
So don't you talk to me about crimes
because for every head I have ever severed
two have grown in their place
and I have had to cut and to cut and to cut
to burn and to cut to purify the world—
understand me?
(*softly*) I killed the Nemean lion
oh yes—
with these hands—with these hands—
and the dog
the dog with the three heads
I collected it from hell in front of the cameras
I have visited the dead in front of the cameras—
remember?
(*Points to himself proudly.*) Kallinikos. Kallinikos.

Pause.

James Yes, Dad.

58

General (*tenderly*) Tell me something: where is my son?

James I am your son.

General James—Jamie.

James Yes.

General But where is the other one? Where is my little one? The one from Gisenyi.

Slight pause.

James (*in disbelief*) Fuck off.

General Where is my little one?

James Fuck off, Dad—that isn't true.

General I want to see him. I want to see Laela.

James That's not true, Dad. That boy is her brother.

General I want to see my son.

James I am your son—I am your only son—that isn't true.

General You are my only son?

James Yes.

General James—Jamie—my only son.

James That's right.

General Then tell me something, Jamie: why is it so quiet here? When is the attack?

James You're at home, Dad.

General I know where I am. And I know what's it's like before the attack. Sometimes it's so quiet you can hear the ants running over your boots. (*Smiles.*)

James (*turning away*) I have to go.

General Then if you love me promise me something. You must promise to talk to the doctors. You will tell the doctors to help me die. You will help me die. You will not allow me to be humiliated. You will talk to the doctors and the doctors will help me die.

Slight pause.

James I can't do that.

General Why? Don't you love your father?

James Of course I love my father—but I also love justice.

General (*smiles*) Justice.

James Yes.

General This is justice.

James Yes—no—no—not this, but—

General But what? To lose my mind?

James You're not losing your mind. You know precisely what you've done.

General I have only ever done what I was instructed to do. And what I was instructed to do . . . (*Becomes uncertain.*) . . . what I was instructed to do . . . This should be in the diary . . . put this in the diary . . .

Slight pause. James observes his father.

James (*cold*) I'll talk to the doctors. Not help you die— I can't be responsible, obviously, for that—but I can talk to the doctors.

General Mmm?

James I said: I will talk to / the doctors.

General You promise me?

James Yes.

General Give me your hand then.

General stretches out his hand. James hesitates. At the same time Laela appears, holding a book and a plate of food. James warily puts his hand into the General's grasp.

And there's something else.

James It's too tight, Dad.

General There's something else.

James That's too tight.

General Something else you must / promise me.

James It's too fucking tight!

General releases him. Laela makes herself comfortable with book and food. She ignores the conversation that follows.

What?

General I want you to take Laela—mmm?

James I don't know what you mean.

General Take Laela—there she is—she's yours—take her. I'm giving her to you and I'm giving you both money—and money—listen—because I have arranged this—for the child. I want you to take Laela, and I want you to be my child's father.

James (*faint laugh*) To be your child's father.

General Those are my instructions.

James I'm not interested in your instructions, Dad.

General Not interested.

James No.

General (*puzzled*) You don't want Laela? Because Laela can make a man feel like a god. (*Slight pause.*) You should've seen her crouching under that tree. I said to her: what are you doing under this tree? She said: I'm fetching water. I said to her: well, excuse me you don't look as if you're fetching water, you look as if you're crouching under a tree. How is that fetching water?—where is your plastic container?—where is the spring? Oh, she said, I don't need a plastic container, I don't need to go to the spring. My father has told me that if I crouch here long enough, in the shade of these leaves, the water will come to me. (*Slight pause.*) I said: then you'll have a long wait, sweetheart. She said: oh no—the water is already here.

Slight pause.

But now she won't even sleep under the same blanket. She thinks I'm a *mende*, don't you? *Unafikiri mimi ni mende.*

No reaction from Laela. He repeats the question in Swahili. No reaction from Laela.

(*Smiles.*) Cockroach. She thinks I'm a cockroach.

Jonathan Who thinks you're a cockroach, General? Not history, I hope. (*Grins.*)

Jonathan has appeared, mobile phone to his ear.

(*into phone*) Yup, yup—I'm in the house—give me two or three minutes—okay?—No, no—keep them outside please—

As he speaks he shakes James's hand with warmth.

Jamie—good to see you. (*into phone*)—What? I said keep them outside unless we need them—yup—yup—excellent.

62

He ends the call and offers his hand to the General,
who simply stares.

And how is the patient? Well rested after his many
labours? (*Slight pause.*) Getting enough fruit? (*Slight
pause.*) Because I have to say the reports pass through
my office—the medical reports land on my desk—in strict
confidence, naturally—and what I read in those reports,
General, is . . . well it's a story of almost super-human
endurance. (*Smiles.*) According to the doctors, this man
shouldn't really be alive at all—should he, Jamie? But
alive is what you are, and being alive have—well I'm
sure you know this—have certain—what?—obligations.
Obligations not only towards the living, but also—and in
your case very much so—obligations towards the dead.

Pause. The General continues to stare.

(*faint laugh*) You realise that's one big fucking African
headache you gave me?

Pause. The General continues to stare.

Big headache, General. Africa. Remember?

James He's not stupid.

Jonathan Not stupid—of course not—forgive me,
James—obviously not stupid, but very very dangerous:
a man, as I've explained to you, whose independent—and
I stress this—whose completely independent actions have
placed my government in a very delicate position. (*faint
laugh*) There were moments when I even started to
believe that indiscriminate murder—General—had been
my own policy. It was Kitty who kept me sane. The man
I love, she said, could never be responsible for such a
thing. Neither could the man I love be responsible—she
said—for protecting the person who is.

He takes a grape from the bowl of fruit, eats it, and smiles at the General.

'Crimes against humanity.'

General (*almost inaudible*) I killed the Nemean lion . . .

Jonathan What's that?

General I killed the Nemean lion.

Jonathan Uh-hu.

General . . . tore off its skin . . .

Jonathan Uh-hu. Very / probably.

General I killed the snake that guarded the tree . . . bore the weight of the earth . . .

Jonathan Uh-hu.

General . . . reached into the tree . . . broke into the garden . . .

Jonathan Uh-hu—very good.

General . . . killed the snake . . . reached into / the tree . . .

Jonathan (*beckoning*) Now I've brought someone with me, General . . .

General . . . reached into the apple tree . . .

Jonathan This is—I'm sorry: I've forgotten your / name.

Iolaos Iolaos—my name is Iolaos.

Jonathan This is—of course it is—Iolaos—

General . . . pulled the apples out of the tree . . .

Jonathan And Iolaos here has volunteered to make the arrest—d'you understand?—which I'd like him to do very calmly, and with the minimum—obviously—of / force.

General Arrest.

Jonathan Exactly.

Pause.

Iolaos Just need to fasten those wrists, General.

Housekeeper, Physiotherapist and Beautician have followed Iolaos into the room and watch. The General stares at him.

Forgive me, General, but I will have to fasten your wrists.

General (*trying to understand*) . . . 'to fasten your wrists' . . .

Iolaos Yes, sir.

Pause.

General And you are . . .?

Iolaos It's me, sir. Iolaos. I've volunteered to take you out to the vehicle. But first I need—I'm sorry but I really do need to fasten your / wrists.

General . . . 'to take me out to the vehicle' . . .

Iolaos That's right, sir.

Pause.

General (*smiles*) So you're a monkey.

Iolaos No, sir. I'm not a monkey. I'm Iolaos. I'm your friend. You saved my life.

General Saved your life? Oh? Why?

Jonathan Get him out of here / please. (*Puts mobile to ear.*)

Iolaos You saved my life. You ran into fire. You carried me—General—across the sand.

The General considers this, then slowly offers his hands to Iolaos who moves forward to fasten them.

Jonathan (*very soft, into mobile*) What?—no—keep them outside, keep them outside—just have the vehicle / ready.

General Wait.

Iolaos freezes.

(*to Jonathan*) And are there cameras?

Jonathan (*to General*) Mmm? (*into mobile*) One moment. (*to General*) Sorry?

General And are there cameras?

Jonathan Of course there are cameras.

General Ask.

Jonathan What?

General Ask.

Jonathan (*into mobile*) Hello?—yup—listen: he wants to know if there are cameras . . . okay, okay . . . excellent . . . (*to General*) Yes, there are cameras—lots of cameras behind the steel fence—cameras / and lights.

General And the gods?

Jonathan (*to General*) What?

General And the gods? Will the gods be watching?

Iolaos The gods are always watching, General.

General Ask. (*Slight pause.*) ASK THEM.

Jonathan (*into mobile*) Okay . . . Now he wants to know . . . Listen: he wants to know about the gods—

66

gods, the gods—yup yup yup yup, obviously. (*to General*) The gods will be watching: you have my word.

The General offers his wrists once more to Iolaos, who fastens them with a plastic strap.

General Then make it tight, Mister Monkey. That's not tight. Tighter. Make it cut.

James Dad? You're / hurting him!

General Make it cut—good—in front of the cameras. Break open my body for the gods. Show me behind glass on television and I will explain on television how I have cleansed—how I have cleansed—how I have cleansed and purified the world. Tighter!

Jonathan (*softly into mobile during preceding speech*) He's been secured—yup—yup—have the vehicle ready . . .

Iolaos (*to James*) You.

General Tighter.

Iolaos Fetch him a blanket.

General Tighter.

Iolaos Fetch him a blanket—let's get this man / out of here.

James (*to Jonathan*) That's hurting him. You / promised me.

General
And I will explain into the microphones
that my labours are at an end
that what I have done
is what I was instructed to do
and what I was instructed to do
was to extract terror like a tooth from its own
  stinking gums.

I will explain
from my own carefully prepared notes
and meticulous diaries
oh yes
oh yes

that I am not the criminal
but the sacrifice
not the criminal
but the sacrifice
not the criminal
but the sacrifice
not the criminal
but the sacrifice
not the criminal
but the sacrifice
not the criminal
but the sacrifice
not the criminal
but the sacrifice
not the criminal
but the sacrifice
not the criminal
but the sacrifice
not the criminal
but the sacrifice
not the criminal
but the sacrifice
not the criminal
but the sacrifice
not the criminal
but the sacrifice

James (*putting a blanket over his shoulders*) Dad?

Iolaos This way, General . . .

James Dad?

Iolaos Come on, sir. Let's go and find those cameras . . .

James Dad? Dad? These straps are hurting . . .

Jonathan Come on, come on: get him outside.

Jonathan (*softly into mobile*) It's fine—yup—yup—he's co-operating and they're coming out now . . . The son is with them: please don't touch the son.

The General allows Iolaos to guide him out, accompanied by James. We hear their voices recede. Jonathan remains in the room, talking into mobile.

(off)
not the criminal
but the sacrifice
not the criminal
but the sacrifice
not the criminal
but the sacrifice
not the criminal
but the sacrifice
not the criminal
but the sacrifice

*Their voices
fade away . . .*

Iolaos (*off*)
Excellent. Mind
the step, General.
Very good . . .

James (*off*)
They're cutting
into him . . .

Iolaos (*off*) Hold
that door for me
—I said hold it—
hold it open . . .

Jonathan Okay,
okay . . . Listen:
tell them we are
unable to com-
ment for reasons
of security but
that a statement
will be issued
later.

Uh-hu, uh-hu—
well I don't care
who's asking—
just tell them that
the operation has
been successful
and that I will
be making a
full statement
later in the after-
noon. Excellent,
excellent.

*Jonathan ends the call. The phone, however, continues
to occupy his attention for some moments more until
he finally looks up to see the women staring at him.
He seems about to speak, but changes his mind and
goes out.*

*Housekeeper, Physiotherapist and Beautician seem
unable to move.*

*The Housekeeper is the first to start clearing up the
room. Beautician joins her and helps. Physiotherapist
goes over to Laela and helps herself to some of the
food on Laela's plate. Laela reads aloud from her book.*

Laela (*reads*) 'I wish I was not of this people. I wish I was dead or still un . . . un . . .' (*Shows word.*)

Physiotherapist Unborn—not born yet.

Laela 'Or still . . . unborn. We are the people. We are the people of iron. We work by day and in the night we grow sick and die. Our babies will be . . . born, will be born with grey hair and god will destroy us.'

Housekeeper (*under breath*) That will do, Laela.

Laela 'Father will not respect son and the son will . . .' despise?

Physiotherapist Despise—that's right—his / father.

Laela 'Will despise his father and hurt his father with cruel words. The children of the people of iron will cheat their parents of what is owed to them, condemn them, and disobey their wishes.'

Housekeeper (*as before*) I said that's enough.

Laela 'Men will turn the cities of other men to dust without reason. Shame and truth will put on white dresses and hiding their . . . beauty from the people will abandon the earth.' (*Slight pause.*) 'They will go / up into—'

Housekeeper Enough now. You can help us clear up this mess.

Laela Clear up the mess? (*Smiles.*) That is *your* job.

James appears, holding the boy in his arms.

A plane passes on its way to the airport.

Notes

13   *blue cards* Soldiers in combat carry blue or yellow cards which set out the rules of engagement.

26   *Tuseme club* 'Tuseme' is Swahili for 'speak out'. In central Africa Tuseme clubs are organised to empower girls and protect them from sexual abuse.

55   *call for fire* In combat, forward observers locate a target using global-positioning technology. They then 'call for fire' from the artillery.

58   *Kallinikos* 'Glorious victor.' Epithet traditionally applied to Herakles.

62   *Unafikiri mimi ni mende* Swahili for 'You think I'm a cockroach.'

64   *Iolaos* Friend of Herakles. When Herakles severed the heads of the Hydra, Iolaos cauterised the neck stumps to prevent the heads growing back.

65   *monkey* Military slang for military policemen, who are despised by the rest of the army.

70   '*I wish I was not of this people*' Laela reads from *Works and Days* by Hesiod, active *c*.700 BC.